MARTIN SECKER & WARBURG

THE FIRST FIFTY YEARS

MARTIN SECKER & WARBURG

THE FIRST FIFTY YEARS

A Memoir by

GEORGE MALCOLM THOMSON

SECKER & WARBURG
LONDON

First published in England 1986 by
Martin Secker & Warburg Limited
54 Poland Street, London W1V 3DF

British Library Cataloguing in Publication Data

Thomson, George Malcolm
Martin Secker & Warburg: the first fifty years: a memoir
1. Publishers and publishing – Great Britain – History – 20th Century
I. Title
070-5'092'4 Z25

ISBN 0-436-52054-0

Typeset in 11/13pt Linotron Bembo by
Rowland Phototypesetting Ltd, Bury St Edmunds, Suffolk
Printed in Great Britain by St Edmundsbury Press,
Bury St Edmunds, Suffolk
Bound by WBC Bookbinders Ltd, Glamorgan
in Wicotex Snowdon supplied
with the compliments of Winter & Co.

Foreword

PERHAPS THE most remarkable aspect of the memoir that follows is the continuity it reveals. Secker & Warburg has been the home of an extraordinarily disparate bunch of publishers: Martin Secker, Fred Warburg, Roger Senhouse, David Farrer, Barley Alison, Tom Rosenthal, John Blackwell and myself. We could hardly any of us be less alike, yet somehow the style, the ideals, the traditions of Secker & Warburg have remained constant.

In this, our fiftieth anniversary year, we will publish new works by Angus Wilson, Günter Grass, Heinrich Böll, Italo Calvino, Umberto Eco, Malcolm Bradbury, David Lodge, Junichiro Tanizaki, Colette, Saul Bellow, J. M. Coetzee and Alberto Moravia. All their names appear in this memoir among the authors who have played a major role in our past, and it is a continuing privilege to have them on the Secker & Warburg list.

Few industries have seemed so threatened in recent years as book publishing. In the 1960s, when I first joined it, seers were confidently predicting that there would be no more books in ten years: the global village would find other ways of telling its tales, recording its history, arguing its philosophy. But it is the seers who have disappeared, and the book that continues to flourish.

As long as there are those who find the novel, the biography, the polemic, the history congenial and effective ways to put forward their ideas, the book will survive. At Secker & Warburg we shall ensure that the best of them are given the opportunity to be read.

PETER GROSE
London, 1986

The publisher is not a soloist of spiritual exertion, but the conductor of the orchestra.

Thomas Mann

They published what they liked and did their weeping in private.

Frank Swinnerton

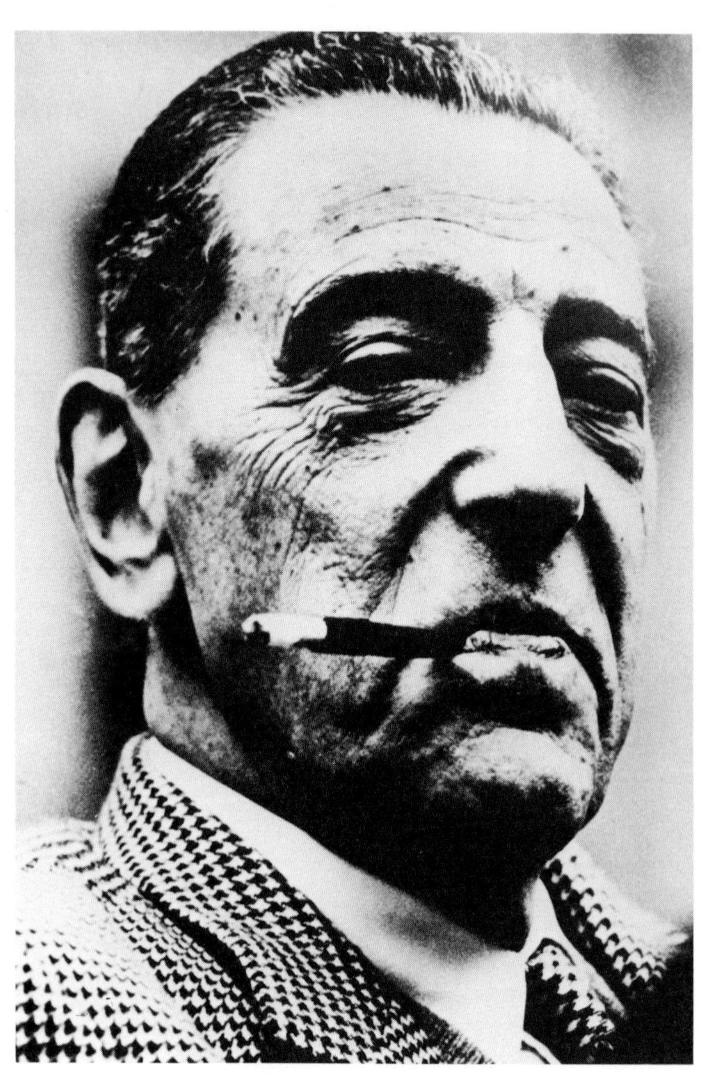

Fredric Warburg (1898–1981)

SOME PUBLISHERS, the best kind of publishers, acquire an easily recognisable style, a personality which remains with them through the years and often survives changes of direction and even of ownership. It would be hard, for instance, to deny that Victor Gollancz, the firm, had an assertive, evangelistic character, as if some Old Testament prophet had stormed out of the desert into Henrietta Street to demand the repentance of a sinful people. In a way, the same is true of Secker & Warburg: the individuality is quite different, more complex, more quirky, but just as strong, imposing itself on each new group of directors and, in turn, picking up from them a measure of fresh colour. After all, no change of direction occurs by accident. The choice of every book reflects to some extent the character of the business. And for those reasons the history of a firm, the list of its publications through the years, becomes a portrait.

A publishing house alters gradually, undergoes modification without ever completely throwing off its original character. Although Martin Secker, who gives his name to half the title of the business, contributed little to the later managing of the company which he sold to

Fredric Warburg half a century ago, it is not fanciful to think that Warburg's period of office, later Rosenthal's, and now Grose's, carries on the tradition which Secker founded. There was a fresh start which was also a continuation.

And what, it may be asked, is the essential nature of Secker & Warburg? How can it be described? Unconventional? That will hardly do. Warburg, although not exactly businesslike, was a professional and thus, in this respect, a conventional publisher; still more was Tom Rosenthal, who *was* businesslike. Quixotic? The adjective suits some of Warburg's doings, and Rosenthal's too, but my own opinion is that the word 'romantic' most comprehensively and yet accurately describes the ethos of the firm. At any rate, it can be agreed that the secret of the business is to be sought in its history which, without any more ado, I now propose to reveal.

If it had not been for Fred Warburg's Aunt Agnes, it is doubtful if the publishing house of Secker & Warburg would have come into being.

In the year 1935, Fredric Warburg had been sacked by the firm of Routledge. It was a disagreeable and unexpected hiccup in a career which up to then had been prosperous. Thirty-six years old, Westminster and Christ Church, an artillery subaltern in the Great War, the bearer of an impressive name, Warburg had risen in thirteen years to be Managing Director of one of the most respected, if somewhat academic, publishing houses in Britain. Now he was suddenly cast out. What made the

Martin Secker (1882–1978)

misfortune all the more tiresome was that he, a divorced man, had recently married a glamorous, strong-minded young woman named Pamela de Bayou. This hitch in his business career came as an unnatural intervention of fate, especially as his first attempts to remedy it ended in failure.

However, he was not easily discouraged. He had determination and a touch of arrogance: he was also, which was less easily noted, imaginative. And he was a Warburg. However, 'The astonishing fact,' he once wrote, 'about the London Warburgs is that they are *poor* Warburgs.' It depends, of course, on what you mean by 'poor'. Certainly Fred did not inherit the family's talent for finance. He had, on the other hand, a highly developed degree of independence and audacity. His quarrel with Routledge arose because, among other innovations, he wished that intensely conservative firm to develop a fiction list. They decided to do without novels, and without Warburg.

There he was then, trudging from one publisher's office to another, looking for the job which, it seemed, nobody wanted to give him, until he had the idea of becoming a publisher on his own – and buying the bankrupt but distinguished firm of Martin Secker Limited, then in the hands of a liquidator.

There was a curious similarity between Warburg's career and Secker's. As a reader for Eveleigh Nash, the latter had read in manuscript a novel he thought highly of. When Nash refused to publish it, Secker set up in publishing on his own and put the novel on his first list in 1910. It was Compton Mackenzie's *The Passionate Elopement*, which was an instant success.

Martin Secker's first book – Compton Mackenzie's *The Passionate Elopement* (1910)

In the twenty-five years that followed, Secker published some of the finest writers of the era: Frank Swinnerton, James Elroy Flecker, Thomas Mann, Franz Kafka, D. H. Lawrence, Lion Feuchtwanger, Hugh Walpole, Norman Douglas . . . a remarkable constellation of talent. Secker was a truly brilliant publisher – and a commercial failure. Why? Warburg thought the reason was lack of capital, a perennial weakness of the publishing trade of which he became more conscious as time passed. It was probably part of the truth. In 1935, the opportunity of buying Secker's name and back-list was just what Warburg needed. The question was, how much would Secker's creditors want – and how was the money to be found? The answer to the first was £5,000. The second appeared at first to be insoluble because the sum was a good deal more than Warburg could put up. It seemed that an impassable gulf yawned between him and the tempting row of unpublished books which would be his if somehow Secker's creditors could be squared. Consider the titles: Erskine Caldwell's *Tobacco Road*, short stories by Thomas Mann and two books by Franz Kafka – a writer who was at that time more respected than read. Finally, there was *Clochemerle*, a novel by an unknown French author, Gabriel Chevallier. Of this unpublished masterpiece, Martin Secker thought well and, as it turned out, was right to do so.

By 15 March 1936, at 3 p.m., the fate of this array of books would be settled, and it was already mid-February. Could it be settled in a way agreeable to Warburg? In the course of conversation, Secker let fall the name of Roger Senhouse, a young man with some money and an enthusiasm for literature, but one who

The last annual catalogue issued by Martin Secker

knew nothing of publishing. A week later Warburg met Senhouse – handsome, cultivated, Eton and Magdalen, Oxford, latest of a long line of landowners from Maryport in Cumberland, and at that time employed in an import–export firm at Hay's Wharf in London's dockland. He had an impressive list of friends in the world of letters, such as Harold Nicolson and Stephen Spender. Even more interesting, he had been the lover – the last lover – of Lytton Strachey. 'His spirit,' says Strachey's biographer, 'so vague and wayward, combining the cross-currents of learning and lasciviousness, lived and moved in a superb uncertainty' (Michael Holroyd, *Lytton Strachey*, Vol. 2).

All that Warburg saw at his first meeting with this 'creature of curious taste and fantasy' were the looks and charm, and that aura of inherited wealth. And, of course, the profound love of literature. It seemed, during those hours of talk, that each complemented the other perfectly although, as it turned out, this was far from being the case.

Over lunch in the Gargoyle Club in Dean Street, Soho, the two reached agreement. Senhouse would put in £3,000 (against the advice of an eminent banker, but with the approval of his fortune-teller) while Warburg with the help of Aunt Agnes was to contribute £1,000. The trouble was that Warburg's aunt, a well-to-do spinster in her sixties, had yet to share the secret. However, there was some reason for optimism. Had not Aunt Agnes already given to the nation that part of Box Hill where George Meredith had lived for some years? Warburg called at the lady's house in Porchester Terrace and stated his case. 'It is probably idiotic to give you the money,' said Aunt Agnes. And did just that.

DEATH IN VENICE

THOMAS MANN

Translated by H. T. Lowe-Porter

LONDON

MARTIN SECKER

NUMBER FIVE JOHN STREET

ADELPHI

Title page of the first UK edition of Thomas Mann's *Death In Venice* (1928)

Senhouse and Warburg put their bid – for £3,000 – in an envelope and took it to the offices of Fairbairn, Wingfield & Wykes, Accountants, Watling Street, Lon-

Portrait of Roger Senhouse (1899–1970) by Clemence Dane. (By courtesy of The Stone Gallery, Burford.)

don EC4. At 3 p.m. Mr Wingfield said, 'I have two bids, each for £3,000. Why don't you raise your offer?' '£3,100,' said Warburg. 'Accepted,' replied Wingfield. At that moment, it may be said, the publishing house of Martin Secker & Warburg came into existence, although where the working capital was going to come from, its enthusiastic founders did not know. Who was going to pay the wages, the rent, the electricity bill, to say nothing of the printers? All these dreary problems were left by Warburg, who knew nothing about finance, to Senhouse, who knew no more. He was a bachelor, as wayward in his own way as Warburg: his charm proved to be a useful quality when it came, as it often did, to conjuring money out of the pockets of trusting friends or repelling importunate creditors. But, of course, charm was not his only quality.

A visit to Roger Senhouse in those days was like something in a page of Balzac. All round the room, waist-high against the walls, are piled the remains of Lytton Strachey's library, bequeathed to Senhouse. Above them hang choice post-Impressionist paintings. And there, sitting at a round rent table, is the Great Lover himself, still handsome if somewhat going to seed, exchanging on the telephone, in French, gossip of the homosexual underworld with a like-minded friend – or listening with marble indifference to a report from the Cumbrian police of the latest burglary at the family mansion. This over, he picks up his pen to continue his translation of *Chéri* – the handwriting is exquisite, the ink purple.

A page of Balzac? With a touch of Huysmans.

As matters turned out, the working capital of the

infant business, installed in new offices at 22 Essex Street, Strand, was £8,300, most of it furnished by Senhouse's friends. Less noticed amid all the flurry of the launch was that the two principals, apparently so different, shared one unfortunate characteristic, a real dislike of money. Amongst the staff inherited from Secker was J. G. Pattisson, a young man with ill-defined but far-ranging managerial responsibilities. Martin Secker himself stayed on in charge of production.

On 4 April 1936 the new firm published its first work, a novel by Elinor Mordaunt entitled, ominously enough, *Prelude to Death.* It had been taken over from Martin Secker. It was not the best time to start a new publishing company – or anything else for that matter. The Abyssinian war was just over; the crucial pre-war event in Europe, the occupation of the Rhineland, had occurred a few weeks before; the persecution of the German Jews had begun. It was reasonable to expect that a new, small enterprise – under-manned, ludicrously under-financed, led by two starry-eyed young men – would come to an early and ignominious end. Something more than a deferential visit to Aunt Agnes in Porchester Terrace would be needed to avert the calamity.

There was also the question of politics, which became more important as time went on. It was the age of Nazism, the Spanish Civil War was a few months off, and the omens of a far greater conflict were already visible. As a proud and loyal Jew, Warburg had declared personal war on the criminal lunatic Hitler; as an intelligent Englishman, he was quick to see through Stalin's treacheries. Thus he was bound to dislike the role being played by a far more prestigious publisher,

PRELUDE TO DEATH

by

ELINOR MORDAUNT

LONDON

MARTIN SECKER

& WARBURG LTD.

1936

The first title published by Martin Secker & Warburg Limited – Elinor Mordaunt's *Prelude to Death* (4 April 1936)

Victor Gollancz, who founded the Left Book Club and made it the most powerful propagandist force in Britain for the Socialist cause. In their orange jackets, the publications of the Club were heralds of a new brand of revolutionary zeal in the minds of young people up and down the land.

Was there room for another, less narrowly based expression of Left opinion, one which did not enjoy the support of the Communist Party? While Fred wondered about this, he was approached by Fenner Brockway, Secretary of the Independent Labour Party, who encouraged him to think that promising young writers of the party would bring him their work. This was tempting, because the new little firm could not thrive on the relics of Martin Secker's list alone.

During the next three years, one-third of the books Secker & Warburg published were definitely of the Left and were hated for their anti-Stalinism by the faithful of the Left Book Club. In Fred Warburg's eyes, Martin Secker & Warburg was at that time not only a publishing company but a 'movement' with a cause which may roughly be called liberal Socialism but was sometimes denounced as Trotskyism by the less intelligent members of the Left. To what extent Senhouse was aware of the role his partner designed for the business for which, after all, he, Senhouse, had found most of the money, is not clear. In any case, Senhouse was fully occupied with the niggling, ever-present problems of finance while Warburg guided the publishing.

At the end of 1936, Secker & Warburg recorded a turnover of £7,618 and a net loss of £3,283, about half the paid-up capital. In his more optimistic moments, Warburg consoled himself with the continuing sale of *Clochemerle*, the lively French novel inherited from Martin Secker, which by the end of the year had sold

Martin Secker & Warburg's first seasonal catalogue

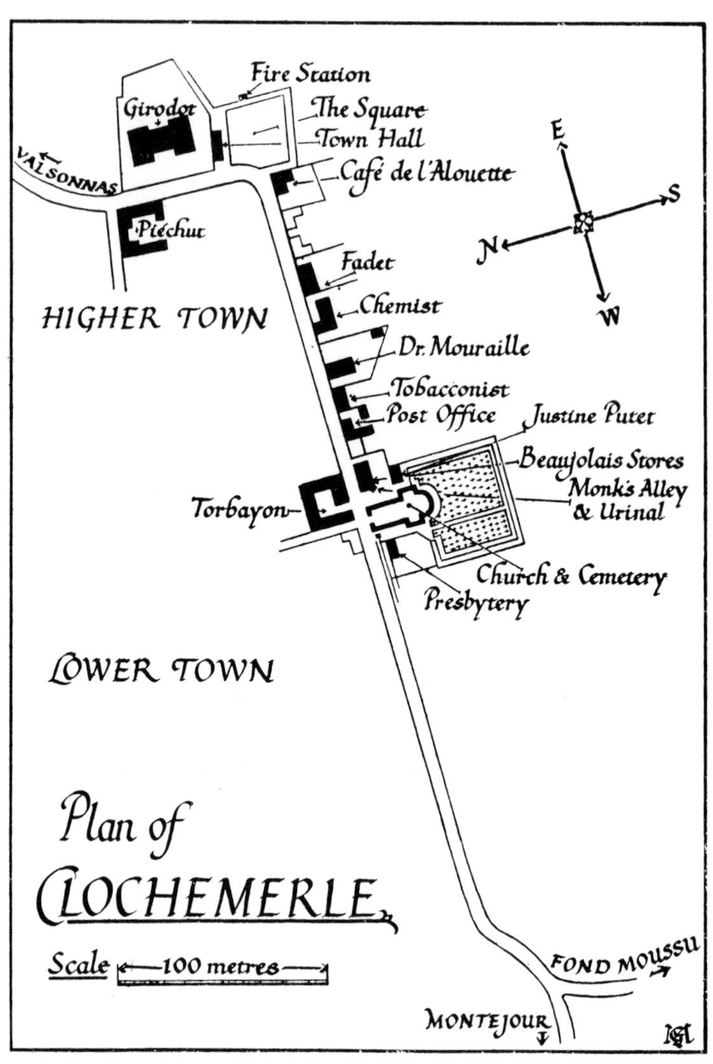

Town plan of the Beaujolais village of Clochemerle, from Gabriel Chevallier's classic comedy (1936)

4,734 copies. It was on its way to far greater things – to sales in one language and another which could be counted in hundreds of thousands. Already it was a gleam of light in what was, admittedly, a rather desolate scene.

In the second year came an eruption of something like civil war among the British Left publishers. André Gide, illustrious French writer and idol of the Left, visited Russia and recorded his observations in *Back from the USSR*. The book made the most painful impression among the faithful: 'The futile outpourings of a decaying homosexual,' they said, and so on. As Roger Senhouse had obtained the British rights to the book from his friend, the author, the anguish of the Left was focused on Secker & Warburg. Warburg's determination to give a political slant to the firm had brought a deluge of abuse but, it seemed, nothing else.

However, George Orwell, a young Socialist author much respected but not, so far, a best-seller, came back from service in the Spanish Civil War shocked by what he had seen of Communist treachery to their comrades. Orwell was one of Victor Gollancz's bevy of left-wing authors, and when Gollancz refused to publish his exposure of the horrible events he had witnessed in Spain, Orwell brought his book, *Homage to Catalonia*, to Secker & Warburg, who published it in 1938. Written in the trenches outside Barcelona when its author was serving in the POUM militia (vaguely Anarchist but politically confused), the book was commercially a failure but it led the way to two publishing triumphs later on.

Others might have recognised Orwell and published him; others might have been glad to pick up that literary

George Orwell (1903–50) by Pamela de Bayou

jewel which Gollancz in his sectarian zeal had rejected. But, in fact, it was Seckers who did so. The relations between author and publisher have often been important – never more so than in the strong personal bond which was forged between Orwell and Warburg and strengthened later when they served together in the Home Guard.

However, though the political sky was stormy, Secker & Warburg published forty books in the second year of its life and an influx of fresh capital helped bolster its flagging economy. The company was beginning to show that it stood for something; it already had a recognisable character, which was shown not simply in its political attitude, which could hardly be mistaken, but more importantly, in the kind of books it published, in their quality, in their flavour.

One sad consequence of the strong political tinge which, under the impulse of Warburg, had been given to the firm was that Martin Secker resigned. As a Tory, he found the wind blowing from the Left too strong. He was interested in literature, not politics. However, the primacy of the company as a publisher of distinguished books translated from the German may be recognised as continuing the original Secker tradition. Responsibility for production was taken over by John Lloyd until the RAF claimed him.

There was a more immediate cause for depression than the threat of war. Money. It seemed that Senhouse could draw no more from his friends. When Warburg suggested to Aunt Agnes that another £5,000 would put the firm on its feet, she referred him to cousin Siegmund, the merchant banker. He, perhaps unable to endure the thought of a Warburg in financial difficulties, produced the money on condition that Hans Lothar, a refugee from Germany, was brought in as a director, with special responsibility for finance. This arrival of reinforcements was, however, not enough to solve the financial problem.

In the meantime, publishing went on as if there was no need to worry about money. Warburg persuaded H. G. Wells to let Secker & Warburg publish eight of his next ten books. Lewis Mumford's *The Culture of Cities* (1938), by any standards a book of the highest importance, was brought to the firm thanks to Warburg's friendship with the author. Its advent might have saved the day financially had it not coincided with the Munich crisis. Its success was postponed. In the last year of peace, the Secker & Warburg imprint was carried by only nineteen books – turnover a miserable £11,855. By July 1939, the £5,000 which Aunt Agnes had advanced with Siegmund's approval had vanished.

Senhouse promised to find another £5,000 but was at first unable to do so although, later that summer, it appears that he did. It is hardly to be wondered at that Warburg momentarily lost his cool and in an outburst of fury dismissed staff right and left. This lapse he later regretted.

On the eve of the war, Secker & Warburg was the publisher of at least seven authors of high distinction (Thomas Mann, Franz Kafka, Lewis Mumford, H. G. Wells, George Orwell, Arnold Zweig and Erskine Caldwell) and was on the brink of disaster, facing its biggest loss: £3,760. Then the long-foreseen storm broke over Europe, changing everything.

War induces people to read and buy more books. It also curtails the supply of the raw materials of publishing – paper and ink. So after a situation in which there were too many books and not enough buyers there followed a crisis of the opposite nature. Warburg, finding himself with money in hand – thanks mainly to the efforts of Senhouse – invested a large proportion of it in paper, which he stored in William Brendon's printing works in Plymouth. It seemed a prudent thing to do.

The firm escaped the London Blitz of 29 December 1940, which destroyed Paternoster Row, the traditional heart of the British book trade, but disaster was only postponed until March 1941. In two successive raids on Plymouth, the premises of William Brendon were wiped out. Two hundred thousand Secker & Warburg books were in ashes, in addition to manuscripts, proofs and twenty tons of paper, the equivalent of two years' ration. It was a shattering blow.

In fact, at first it seemed to be fatal. But one day while Warburg was gloomily contemplating the ruins of their fortunes, the angel of deliverance walked into his office. He was Mr Norrington, a representative of the famous Edinburgh printing firm, Morrison & Gibb. Having heard the tale of catastrophe, Norrington told Warburg that the head of Morrison & Gibb had locked away 2,000 tons of paper, some of which might be available for just such an emergency as this. So the sun shone again. In spite of the *Luftwaffe*, Secker & Warburg were still in business. In fact, the paper crisis was never so severe again.

In 1941 and 1942 the firm made good profits. Between 1941 and 1944 it published Edmund Wilson's *To the Finland Station* (1941) and *The Wound and the Bow* (1942), Henry Miller's *The Colossus of Maroussi* (1942) and John Prebble's *Where the Sea Breaks* (1944). Plainly Secker & Warburg was maintaining its reputation as a firm which could surprise as well as please the public. Then, one night in August 1944, came the second and, it seemed, the mortal blow. A flying bomb destroyed the building in Essex Street, which contained the business records of the company, the carbon copies of letters and contracts, the office furniture and the typewriters. Contemplating the rubble in the early dawn next day, Warburg espied a dust-covered figure engaged in rescue work: Senhouse. 'You find an office,' said Senhouse. 'I'm busy here.' Two months later, the firm moved to 7 John Street, Bloomsbury, which was to be its home for the next seventeen years.

A year after this disaster, Secker & Warburg published one of its most important books, 'a little squib which may amuse you when it comes out', as its author described it. *Animal Farm*, as it was called, is, like *Gulliver's Travels*, an amusing fable; it was also dynamite. George Orwell, who conceived it and, after six years, wrote it, launched it as a deadly missile against Soviet Communism, which he regarded as a dangerous perversion of Socialism, a false creed being disseminated by the most powerful propagandist machine on earth.

The manuscript of *Animal Farm* was rejected by Gol-

A selection of signatures of Secker & Warburg authors

lancz, Faber and Cape. Orwell, undaunted, declared that he was willing to publish it at his own expense, as a pamphlet, price two shillings.

Instead, he brought it to Warburg, who read it, as did Senhouse. Both had no doubt that they had a masterpiece on their hands. They would publish, Senhouse being even more convinced than his partner. To do so called for more courage than may now appear: the book was far too short and the theme was politically untimely – an attack on Russia at a time when Russia was fighting with such heroism! There were, then, literary, political and even diplomatic arguments against publication. As it turned out, the war was over by the time the book was issued in August 1945. Advance to the author: £100; American rights sold for £250. Thirty years later, nine million copies of *Animal Farm* had been sold in one country or another, in one language or another. It was the most sensational success the firm had registered up to that time. It was, however, not the only one.

Among the correspondence rescued by Senhouse from the bomb wreckage in Essex Street was a sheaf of letters between him and Edwin Muir concerning a project for publishing a collected edition of the works of Franz Kafka. Muir, an Orcadian, was a thoughtful man with a great deal of quiet charm. His reputation as a poet of high distinction is now securely established but, in the thirties, he was chiefly known as a translator from the German and a perceptive observer of the German literary scene. He and his wife, Willa, worked as a translating team. Kafka's novel, *The Castle*, and the stories issued under the title *The Great Wall of China* were among the properties taken over from Martin Secker in 1936. Although neither had sold well, there were signs by 1940 that public interest in Kafka was growing. In some way he seemed to correspond to the thought and frustrations of the new age. Senhouse, in particular, was eager to produce a definitive Kafka edition. But the difficulties were enormous. To begin with, there was the embarrassing fact that Kafka had given his executor, Max Brod, instructions to destroy all his unpublished works – and Brod believed them to be masterpieces! Brod, a man with a

The definitive edition of Franz Kafka's
The Trial (1945)

conscience, was in a dilemma. The war and the dispersion of the European Jews were contributory factors in what became an almost baffling problem. Who owned the copyrights of these works? Where was the mysterious proprietor? Unable to answer the first question, Warburg and Senhouse publicly announced that they controlled all the British rights in Kafka's work. This was bold, but untrue.

After a prolonged search, the owner of the copyrights was found to be Mr Salman Schocken, a German–Jewish businessman, whose life was divided between Tel-Aviv and New York. When Schocken came to London, he failed to reach rapport with Senhouse and complained, reasonably enough, that Secker & Warburg had used his copyrights without permission or payment. Such was his indignation that he was apparently on the verge of taking the books to another British publisher. However, the tortuous skein was in due course smoothed out; Mr Schocken read Warburg a final lecture on business ethics, and in 1945 a definitive edition of *The Trial* was published, with other Kafka works to follow. Secker & Warburg was firmly in possession of the right to publish a European master, as great at least as Thomas Mann.

By the end of the war the firm was established in every way but financial, and its essential character was recognised: quality with a touch of waywardness. As for its financial troubles, it seemed that these would never be satisfactorily dealt with so long as Fredric Warburg remained shy of reality – believing, it seemed, that it would always be possible to bring in fresh partners who would also be new investors. Nor was this as crazy as it sounds. Secker & Warburg was undoubtedly distinguished; there was no obvious reason why it should not prosper if properly managed, and certainly no reason why it could not attract fresh talent.

In the autumn of 1946, a new executive was introduced: David Farrer, a product of Rugby and Balliol and a member of a Yorkshire family distinguished in the law. During the war, Farrer had served in Lord Beaverbrook's

David Farrer (1906–83)

Jacket illustration from the 1986 reissue of
Milton Shulman's *Defeat in the West*,
first published in 1947

secretariat in various ministries. His ability was not in doubt, nor was his thoughtful, kindly nature. Among the other gifts he brought with him to Seckers was an instinctive, sensitive understanding of the nature of authors. To David a writer was a human being, probably in some kind of trouble, to be approached delicately, with tact and affection. Nobody could be more likely than he to continue and strengthen the essential character of the firm.

With him, as it chanced, Farrer brought a book, *Defeat in the West* (1947), by a Canadian intelligence officer, Milton Shulman. The book was, in fact, the first study of the war as it had been seen by the leading German generals. It was of absorbing interest in those immediate post-war months. It sold well and rightly brought great kudos to its promoter, Farrer, who until then had had no experience of publishing. The book is still in great demand and is now reprinting with an introduction by Max Hastings.

In the immediate post-war phase, when some of the limitations of production were still in force, Secker & Warburg was as active as it could be in the circumstances. The company launched, under the general title of Sigma Books, a new series on the latest advances in science, and in April 1946 a new novel by Gabriel Chevallier, *Sainte-Colline*, appeared. The pace of publishing quickened throughout the months that followed. However, the outstanding event of this period for the firm happened on 8 June 1949. On this date George Orwell's last and most sensational book burst on the public – the political novel which, after some hesitation, he called *Nineteen Eighty-Four*.

From the famous first sentence – 'It was a bright cold day in April and the clocks were striking thirteen' – Orwell's novel set out to destroy what he thought of as the most dangerous delusion of the age: the belief that the totalitarian state was a benevolent system. With this purpose in mind he mobilised a whole array of novel concepts which have since passed into the currency of everyday speech, including Ingsoc, unperson, Big Brother, Thought Police and the Ministry of Truth (with its slogans: 'War is Peace', 'Freedom is Slavery', 'Ignorance is Strength'). The invention was brilliant, the theme unspeakably chilling. On that June day in 1949, Secker & Warburg gave the world one of the key books of the century. That Seckers and not another publishing house issued it testified to one quality of the small, independent firm: it could act quickly and decisively.

Nineteen Eighty-Four was the work of a man who was stricken with tuberculosis, and in fact died seven months later. He brought the book to Seckers because, as he explained to Gollancz, Secker & Warburg had published *Animal Farm*, and anyone who would risk *that* book would risk anything! The risks, at that moment in history, appeared to be far from trifling.

When it first appeared, *Nineteen Eighty-Four* aroused the intense hostility of some reputable critics. Why? At the time, I said in a review in the *Evening Standard*, 'because its impact has such power, violence and lucidity'. (It is not often that one can read with pleasure something one wrote forty years ago!) Now it seems self-evident that partisan dislike would not prevent the book's success. But that is to forget the power and pervasiveness of the Marxist mythology in 1949. In fact, the book went off, as high explosives do, with a bang. The hostile critics (Priestley, Frank O'Connor, Shanks) snarled in vain.

Two months before Orwell's last book appeared, Secker & Warburg introduced the public to an important new writer of fiction, Angus Wilson. Angus, at the time Deputy Superintendent of the Reading Room at the British Museum, sent some short stories to his friend John Pattisson (now returned to publishing from the

1.

It was a cold, blowy day in early April, and a million radios were striking thirteen. Winston Smith pushed open the glass door of Victory Mansions, turned to the right down the passage-way and pressed the button of the lift. Nothing happened. He had just pressed a second time when a door at the end of the passage opened, letting out a smell of boiled greens and old rag mats, and the aged prole who acted as porter and caretaker thrust out a grey, seamed face and stood for a moment sucking his teeth and watching Winston malignantly.

"Lift ain't working," he announced at last.

"Why isn't it working?"

"The lifts ain't working. The currents is cut orf at the main. The 'eat ain't working neither. All currents to be cut orf during daylight hours. Orders!" he barked in military style, and slammed the door again, leaving it uncertain whether the grievance he evidently felt was against Winston, or against the authorities who had cut-off the current.

Winston remembered now. It was part of the economy drive in preparation for Hate Week. The flat was seven flights up, and Winston, conscious of his thirty-nine years and of the varicose ulcer above his right ankle, rested at each landing to avoid putting himself out of breath. On every landing the same poster was gummed to the wall - a huge coloured poster, too large for indoor display. It depicted simply an enormous face, the face of a man of about forty-five, with ruggedly handsome features, thick black hair, a heavy moustache and

Facsimile of the first page of the manuscript of George Orwell's *Nineteen Eighty-Four* (1949)

Jacket by Ronald Searle for Angus Wilson's
Anglo-Saxon Attitudes (1956)

Tank Regiment). Their originality of temper was immediately obvious. The first collection was published in March 1949 under the title *The Wrong Set*. It was followed by *Such Darling Dodos* (1950) and a novel, *Hemlock and After* (1952). A substantial new talent, a writer with the stamp of genius, had arrived on the scene and Secker & Warburg had the perception to recognise it. If any individual member of the firm deserves especial praise for this perception, it is David Farrer. 'On the censorship borderline,' he reported on the first Wilson typescript, '. . . a likely candidate for big sales.' These began to come with Wilson's first novel, *Hemlock and After*, which sold 12,000 copies in its first year (many good judges believe it to be Wilson's best novel). But still bigger sales lay ahead.

John Prebble was another writer of distinction added to the firm's list during the last months of war and the first years of peace. While serving as a lance-corporal with a radar unit, he had written his first novel, *Where the Sea Breaks*, which was published in July 1944 and quickly sold 10,000 copies. Two other novels followed, after which Prebble found what seemed to be his true vein: studies of events, usually tragic, in the Scottish past – the Highland Clearances, the Massacre of Glencoe etc. His obsession with Scotland was strange in a way, for his birthplace was in Canada and his roots were in Kent. But his upbringing among exiled Scots in Saskatchewan had infected him with their nostalgia. In addition, he possessed an emotional sympathy with defeated people which lent to his writing an intensity greater than mere narrative power. In describing Culloden, he found himself gradually committed to unfolding the whole tragic panorama of the Scottish story.

The Highland Clearances (1963) by John Prebble

One of the earliest consequences of the end of the war was the re-opening of American business. Warburg was soon on the trail westward.

From a trip to New York in 1947, the 'golden year' as Warburg called it, he brought back Lionel Trilling's novel, *The Middle of the Journey* (1948), based on the careers of Alger Hiss and Whittaker Chambers, and John Horne Burns' first volume, *The Gallery* (1948), an exposure of wartime Naples at its sleaziest.

The next expedition in 1951 produced James A. Michener's *Return to Paradise*, bought for £350 and before

RETURN TO

Paradise

by

JAMES A. MICHENER

LONDON SECKER & WARBURG 1951

Title page of the first James A. Michener book published by Secker & Warburg – *Return to Paradise* (1951) long a publishing success. In the same year, an ambition to publish a succession of Colette's novels – nurtured, above all, by Senhouse – was carried an important step forward by the appearance of *Chéri*. All told, Seckers published twenty-one books by this Frenchwoman of genius.

But at this point in the story it is necessary to turn to more sombre affairs. The wind of inflation was rising, costs of every kind were mounting fast. By the spring of 1951, Secker & Warburg was running out of money. This was the chilling news Farrer conveyed to Warburg on the Waterloo Station platform when Warburg returned from his latest foray in New York.

In spite of its undoubted prestige, its publishing of authors of worldwide fame, its occasional runaway successes (*Clochemerle*, *Nineteen Eighty-Four*), Seckers could not carry on much longer without some radical transformation. This sad truth was seen with particular clarity by Farrer, the most realistic of its directors and the one with the most practical approach to the problem. Having discussed the matter with Warburg, Farrer put the ugly facts before his friend A. S. Frere, head of William Heinemann. From this move there eventually emerged, in 1951, a generous and sensible collaboration between the two firms. Heinemann took over distribution and sales, and agreed to guarantee an overdraft (which in due course was more than £100,000). Secker & Warburg was to keep complete editorial independence, on condition that no advance on a book exceeded £300. The arrangement was successful, the fears of the pessimists proved to be unfounded: 'You'll be turned into just another department of that huge production machine,' one literary

ENCOUNTER

LITERATURE ARTS POLITICS

AFTER THE APOCALYPSE
The Editors

PAGES FROM A DIARY *Virginia Woolf*

LOOKING FOR INDIA *Denis de Rougemont*

THE WIND AT DJEMILA *Albert Camus*

THE HEAD OF A LEADER *Christopher Isherwood*

A POSTSCRIPT TO THE ROSENBERG CASE *Leslie A. Fiedler*

TWO STORIES *Dazai Osamu*

POEMS BY *Dr. Edith Sitwell* AND *C. Day Lewis*

MARK ALEXANDER J. K. GALBRAITH NATHAN GLAZER
IRVING KRISTOL ALBERTO de LACERDA NICOLAS NABOKOV
TOM SCOTT HUGH SETON-WATSON STEPHEN SPENDER

OCTOBER 1953 1 MONTHLY 2s. 6d.

Cover of the first issue of *Encounter* magazine
(October 1953)

Jacket from the first edition of John Wain's *Hurry on Down* (1953)

agent had warned. Not so. Basically, the success of the collaboration sprang from the friendly relation which existed between Frere and Farrer and, in due course, grew up between Frere and Warburg.

In 1955 there was a surprising incident: Warburg paid an £800 advance for what purported to be the autobiography of a Tibetan lama called T. Lobsang Rampa. The advance was large, the story told in the manuscript was extraordinary. Among other wonders, it described how the Dalai Lama submitted Lobsang Rampa to a surgical operation known as the opening of the third eye, designed to increase his powers of clairvoyance. Warburg read the manuscript with mounting enthusiasm but was doubtful – the book was either a true account of mysterious goings-on in Tibet or it was a farrago of nonsense. In the end, after prolonged discussion and in the face of strong reservations in several quarters, it was published as *The Third Eye* (1956), with a preface announcing that the author bore sole responsibility for the statements in it.

In fact, as duly emerged, the 'Tibetan monk' was Cyril Henry Hoskins, the son of a Devon plumber who had never been nearer to Tibet than London. *The Third Eye* was an elaborate hoax aimed first of all at its publishers. In spite of this tardy discovery, the book had sold over 10,000 hardcover copies by the end of 1959. Some people still believe in its authenticity.

Some time before the affair of the lama, a different kind of crisis blew up. The firm had published a novel called *The Philanderer* (1953) which a young policeman in the Isle of Man thought should be prosecuted for obscene libel. The novel had no particular distinction and was, on any reasonable judgement, unlikely to corrupt anybody's morals. However, no publisher had ever been

Not Guilty !

In 1954 this book was the subject of a prosecution at The Old Bailey in which the Publishers and Printers were charged with publishing an obscene libel.

In the course of a notable summing-up, Mr. Justice Stable said :

"The theme of this book is the story of a rather attractive young man who is absolutely obsessed with his desire for women. It is not presented as an admirable thing, or a thing to be copied. It is not presented as a thing that brought him happiness or any sort of permanent satisfaction. Throughout the book you hear the note of impending disaster. He is like the drunkard who cannot keep away from drink, although he knows where it will land him in the end. So far as his amatory adventures are concerned, the book does deal, with candour or, if you prefer it, crudity, with the realities of human love and human intercourse. There is no getting away from that, and the Crown say : 'Well, that is sheer filth.'

"Members of the jury, is it ? Is the act of sexual passion sheer filth ? It may be an error of taste to write about it. It may be a matter in which perhaps old-fashioned people would mourn the reticence that was observed in these matters yesterday. But is it sheer filth ? That is a matter, members of the jury, you have to consider and ultimately to decide."

The jury of nine men and three women returned a verdict of

NOT GUILTY

Mr. Justice Stable's summing up is included in this edition and can also be obtained in pamphlet form from any bookseller or direct from the publishers for one shilling.

The Philanderer (1953) by Stanley Kauffman, acquitted of the charge of obscene libel

acquitted when faced with this charge. The outlook for Secker & Warburg was, therefore, by no means bright.

Frere, Managing Director of Heinemann, was in no doubt what should be done: take your medicine; it's less dangerous. But Warburg, a stubborn man, decided to fight. Very sensibly; the judge told the Old Bailey jury to go away and read the book. They did so and decided that the general effect of *The Philanderer* was not immoral. Secker & Warburg was acquitted. After the trial, the novel sold 20,000 copies to a public which was deeply disappointed by its contents.

1936-1961

SECKER & WARBURG

celebrate the 25th anniversary of the firm (incorporating Martin Secker Ltd) and recall with pride a few of their famous books:

DAVID BEATY The Proving Flight
PIERRE BOULLE The Bridge on the River Kwai
GABRIEL CHEVALLIER Clochemerle
COLETTE Cheri · Gigi
ANDRE GIDE Strait is the Gate · The Journals, etc.
FRANZ KAFKA The Trial · The Castle
JOMO KENYATTA Facing Mount Kenya
ANDRE MALRAUX The Voices of Silence
THOMAS MANN Dr. Faustus · Felix Krull
JAMES A. MICHENER Hawaii
ARTHUR MILLER The Misfits
EDGAR MITTELHOLZER The Kaywana Trilogy
ALBERTO MORAVIA A Woman of Rome
LEWIS MUMFORD The City in History (Sept '61)
ROBERT MUSIL The Man Without Qualities
GEORGE ORWELL 1984 · Animal Farm
ANDRE SCHWARZ-BART The Last of the Just
WILLIAM L. SHIRER The Rise and Fall of the Third Reich
LIONEL TRILLING The Liberal Imagination
TENNESSEE WILLIAMS Cat on a Hot Tin Roof, etc.
ANGUS WILSON Anglo-Saxon Attitudes · The Wrong Set

Among our younger writers we are proud to publish:

MALCOLM BRADBURY
CHRISTINE BROOKE-ROSE
JAN CAREW
BRIAN GLANVILLE
ROBERT KEE
ERIC NEWBY
FRANK NORMAN
JOHN PREBBLE
JAMES PURDY
TOM STACEY

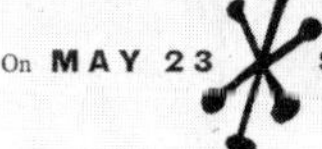

On **MAY 23** **SECKER & WARBURG** will move into new premises at **14 CARLISLE STREET · SOHO SQUARE · W1**

TELEPHONE GERRARD 2078 · 4 LINES

Advertisement placed in the *Times Literary Supplement* to celebrate the twenty-fifth anniversary of the company, April 1951

The Rise and Fall of the Third Reich by William L. Shirer (1960)

Among the brilliant young novelists whom Secker & Warburg introduced to the public during the next few years was Melvyn Bragg (*For Want of a Nail*, 1965) who, in David Farrer, found a congenial editor. 'The reason why you trusted him,' wrote Bragg, 'was that he saw the intention and sympathised, he read the execution and wanted to help.' Bragg's work published by Secker & Warburg, both fiction and non-fiction, formed an important phase in his career.

In 1960, William L. Shirer's *The Rise and Fall of the Third*

Günter Grass's own design for the jacket of *The Tin Drum* (1962)

Reich was published. This big profit-maker was bought by David Farrer on his first visit to New York as a publisher after a brief exchange with Warburg by cable, which went as follows:

WARBURG: 'Don't buy Shirer.'
FARRER: 'Have bought Shirer.'

It is sadly true that Warburg in his autobiography says nothing of those telegrams and does not give Farrer the credit he deserves for what was certainly a major coup – a book which sold over 50,000 copies in six months.

Faithful to its traditional role as the leading English publisher of European books, Secker & Warburg brought out Günter Grass's first novel, *The Tin Drum*, in 1962. It came into the firm's ken through a chance remark to Farrer by Tom Maschler, who was later to join Jonathan Cape Limited. It was an imaginative satire on a huge scale (250,000 words) and was one of the most important works of the post-war era. Another German novel of the highest calibre, Robert Musil's *The Man Without Qualities*, had appeared (in translation) on Secker & Warburg's list in 1953 (volumes 2 and 3 appeared in 1954 and 1960). This masterpiece still awaits the success it deserves.

One day in 1967, Barley Alison joined the firm. This lady, an Australian, had been an officer with the Special Operations Executive during the war and had afterwards spent ten years in the Diplomatic Service. Now she was a distinguished editor who had been for twelve years with Weidenfeld & Nicolson, in which firm she had shares. She wanted a change. In addition, Weidenfeld needed her shares to enable him to raise more capital while retaining a controlling interest in the business.

The terms on which Barley Alison joined Secker & Warburg were as follows: she would find and edit the books to be published under her imprint (The Alison Press); Secker & Warburg would accept the books unless

THE MAN WITHOUT QUALITIES

a novel

by

ROBERT MUSIL

★

Volume I

A SORT OF INTRODUCTION

THE LIKE OF IT NOW HAPPENS (I)

Volume I of Robert Musil's unfinished masterpiece, *The Man Without Qualities* (1953)

they felt extremely pessimistic about their prospects and would pay all costs of production, including the author's advance. Barley Alison was to receive no salary but would have a good share of the profits, if any. It was a novel arrangement and, to the immense credit of both parties, it has worked.

One of the earliest novels published by The Alison Press was Piers Paul Read's *The Junkers* (1968), which

Nobel prizewinner Saul Bellow's *Humboldt's Gift* (1975), published by The Alison Press in association with Secker & Warburg

George Weidenfeld had given her as a leaving present. Many others have followed over the years. For example, Saul Bellow's seventh novel, *Humboldt's Gift* (1975), was the first of several books by this distinguished writer that bore the imprint of the Press. There have also been seventeen immensely popular sea stories by Dudley Pope, generally regarded as the successor to C. S. Forester in this vein, and, so far, five titles by David Cook have appeared since The Alison Press first published *Albert's Memorial* in 1972.

The arrival of Barley Alison on the scene brought a fresh mind and a new vivacity to the business. Warburg said of her, 'She likes looking after her authors as a mother her children. She is, in my view, God's gift to a needy author struggling to gain a reputation without starving to death.'

The arrangement with Barley Alison was an example of the growing importance of the editor as publishing became concentrated into larger units. Increasing size brought with it the possibility of a weakening of the personal link between an author and his publisher. The link between author and editor would, however, remain and might even be strengthened. Authors would feel a loyalty to an editor they liked – David Farrer being a shining example of this – and might even follow him if he went from one house to another.

When Secker & Warburg – itself an independent associate of the Heinemann Group – entered its carefully defined partnership with a newly formed Alison Press, it was adjusting the traditional individualism of publishing to the new economic conditions of book production. Roughly speaking, there was a division between the imaginative side of publishing and the industrial or commercial. The Alison Press was an attempt to recognise and overcome this dichotomy. Later on, a similar arrangement was made with Leo Cooper, a specialist in books of military interest.

Julian Thompson's account of the Falklands War, *No Picnic* (1985), published by Leo Cooper in association with Secker & Warburg

Twinkling in the firmament of those Warburg and Farrer sixties, one of the brightest new stars was Malcolm Bradbury, casting a sardonic – not to say savage – eye over the smart radicalism of the far-from-peaceful groves of academe. After *Eating People is Wrong* (1959) – bought by Fred Warburg on David Farrer's advice – and *Stepping Westward* (1965) came *The History Man* (1975), acclaimed as a masterpiece and, beyond doubt, one of the most ruthless satires of the time. His appalling hero, Howard Kirk, is a wholly fictitious figure whose like could be met on a dozen trendy campuses then, and not only in the equally fictitious University of Watermouth.

Secker & Warburg had also published, by this time, a representative selection of modern Japanese writers. One of them, Yasunari Kawabata, was awarded the Nobel Prize for Literature in 1968. But he was not by any means the only one of his nation to bring distinction to the Secker list. There was also, for instance, Yukio Mishima.

There must, at this point, be some special mention of two of Christy Brown's books, the autobiography, *My Left Foot* (1954), and the novel, *Down All The Days* (1970), not simply because they are a chapter in the Secker story but because they are a triumph of the human spirit. Brown, a Dubliner, was dreadfully crippled and could write only with his foot. His speech was incoherent, almost incomprehensible. That he wrote at all was a feat of heroism on his part and of faith and patience on the part of his editor, David Farrer. 'To see David encourage him and communicate with him,' Tom Rosenthal was to write in David's obituary, 'was to witness a miracle of tact and compassion and love that testified to the rare and indomitable human qualities of both author and editor.' It was a wonder that Christy Brown could communicate; David Farrer was the wonder-worker.

Towards the close of the sixties, a new crisis overtook Secker & Warburg. Fred Warburg was past retirement age, and his chosen successor, Maurice Temple Smith, resigned over a difference of opinion about the future character of the business. It was necessary to do some-

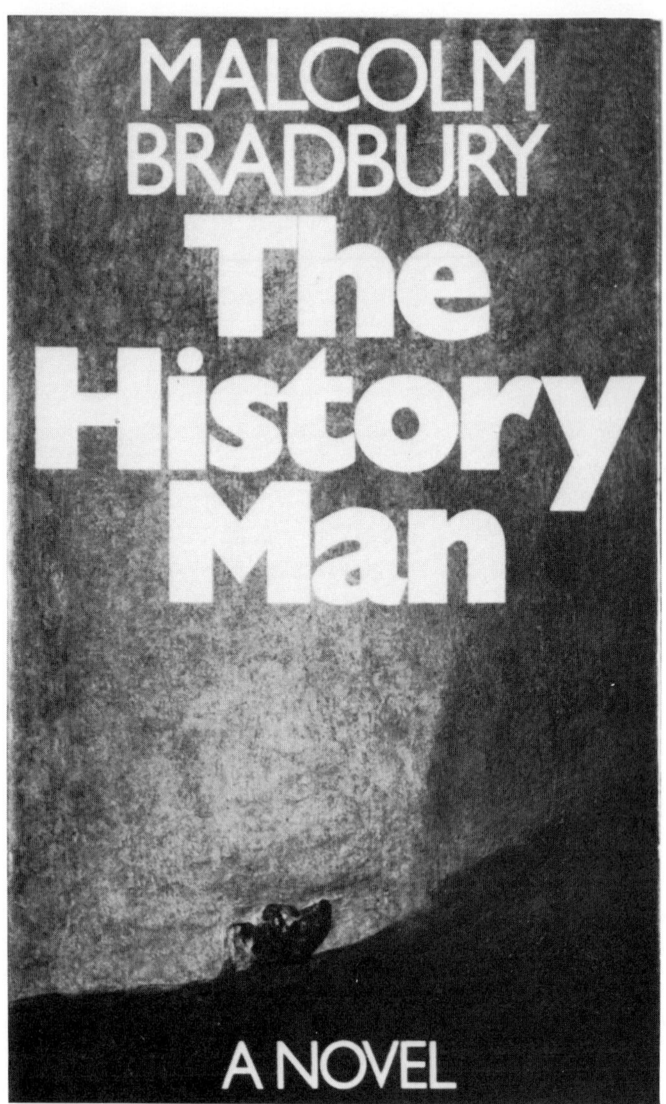

Malcolm Bradbury's widely acclaimed novel, *The History Man* (1975)

thing without delay because, beyond the other reasons for anxiety loomed the familiar problem of finance – Secker & Warburg had lost money for five successive years.

Tillings, the financial group which then owned Heinemann, had a clear idea of what they wanted to do: retire Fred Warburg and find a new Managing Director. There was a brief flurry when Warburg, having been asked to retire, approached Jonathan Cape Limited, who were interested in acquiring the firm. However when this was reported to Heinemann directors, the plan was firmly thrown out. Charles Pick, then Managing Director of Heinemann, felt strongly that the identity of Secker & Warburg had to be preserved, and that with the right management profits could match the high literary reputation the company had always enjoyed.

Pick had already met and been impressed by a young publisher called Tom Rosenthal, then Managing Director of Thames & Hudson International, the international division of the art and illustrated publishers, and felt he might be the right man for the job. However the first approach came through Alan Hill, head of Heinemann Educational and an old friend of Rosenthal. Rosenthal had just come back from a business trip to New York when he had the telephone call from Hill: would he come to lunch at the Garrick Club? Rosenthal accepted, thinking that Hill probably had some business motive. In this, of course, he was right. After a few pleasantries, Hill said, 'You are one of those young men who knows everything that is going on among the young in publishing. Can you help me? We need a replacement for Fred Warburg who will soon be seventy-two, and is way past the normal retirement age. Do you know anyone who might be

SEARCHLIGHT

BOOKS

A KNOCKOUT THRILLER

MERCURY BOOKS
LONDON

A selection of logos used by Martin Secker and Secker & Warburg

suitable?' 'Alan,' said Rosenthal, 'if you are offering me the job, I would like to take it.' Hill was mildly surprised. However, he said, 'Well, yes, as a matter of fact, that was the general idea.'

Rosenthal then presented his terms for accepting the job, lucidly and in good order: he was prepared to take a sizeable cut in salary in order to achieve his ambition of becoming a publisher of fiction, something he could not hope to do with Thames & Hudson; in addition, he wished to be part-owner of the business. This latter condition turned out to be a difficult hurdle, because Thomas Tilling Limited, who owned Heinemann, were opposed, as a matter of principle, to chief executives of subsidiary companies – such as Secker & Warburg – owning shares in the subsidiaries. Some months of discussion were needed before Charles Pick was able to persuade Tillings to make an exception in favour of Rosenthal who, thus, on 1 January 1971, became Managing Director of Secker & Warburg.

No doubt Rosenthal, when he assumed responsibility for this firm, with its glamorous list and its shaky finances, had the notion that he would transform the scene. But it seemed that the tide had already turned. The success of two major books, Christy Brown's *Down All The Days* and Angus Wilson's *The World of Charles Dickens* (1970) had put Seckers modestly into profit before his arrival. It was a rare burst of sunshine which, in time, Rosenthal turned into the normal financial climate.

During the years of his tenure, the turnover of the company rose from a quarter of a million pounds to two and three-quarter millions. Its profit was comfortably in excess of £300,000, making it, as he and Farrer were soon able to boast, *pro rata* the most profitable constituent company of the Heinemann Group. Rosenthal possessed the gift which had eluded previous heads of the firm; as one of his directors said later, 'he knew how and where to save money'. It was a prosaic virtue, but a vital one. It was not Rosenthal's only talent. In addition to being a first-class businessman, he possessed that mysterious gift known as flair. He had the wisdom, too, to recognise what a jewel he had in David Farrer, and to put Barley Alison on the board.

During his term of office, a geographical change also occurred. Secker & Warburg which, since its move from Bloomsbury, had been directed from 14 Carlisle Street, Soho, now moved once more, this time round the corner to 54 Poland Street, on 1 March 1978. Unusual among publishers, it became the owner of its premises.

In the Rosenthal years, more than two hundred new authors were added to the Secker & Warburg list, forming a varied but, on the whole, highly distinguished collection. There was, for example, George V. Higgins' first novel, *The Friends of Eddie Coyle* (1972), in which the Boston Assistant District Attorney broke into the world of crime fiction with a book that in due course became a film. In the following year came Heinrich Böll's novel *Group Portrait with Lady*, the first book by this Nobel prize-winner to appear under the Secker & Warburg imprint. In 1973 two *Washington Post* journalists, Carl Bernstein and Bob Woodward, produced their joint

Group Portrait with Lady (1973) by Nobel prizewinner Heinrich Böll

account of the investigations which led them to unravel the Watergate affair. This sensational journalistic coup led eventually to the fall of President Nixon. The narrative, entitled *All the President's Men* (1974), was published in Britain by Secker & Warburg. In the months that followed, three noteworthy novels appeared: Italo Calvino's *Invisible Cities* (1974), the fifth work of fiction by an

The last book by Italo Calvino published in English during the author's lifetime – *Mr Palomar* (1985)

outstanding Italian writer; David Lodge's *Changing Places* (1975), which won the Hawthornden Prize and the *Yorkshire Post* Fiction Prize; and Maurice Leitch's *Stamping Ground* (1975), a controversial novel set in County Antrim. Leitch went on to win the Whitbread Fiction Prize with his next book, *Silver's City* (1981). In 1977, J. M. Coetzee's *In the Heart of the Country* appeared on the list, the first publication by Secker & Warburg of this

Small World (1984) by David Lodge

Life & Times of Michael K by J. M. Coetzee which won the Booker-McConnell Prize for Fiction in 1983

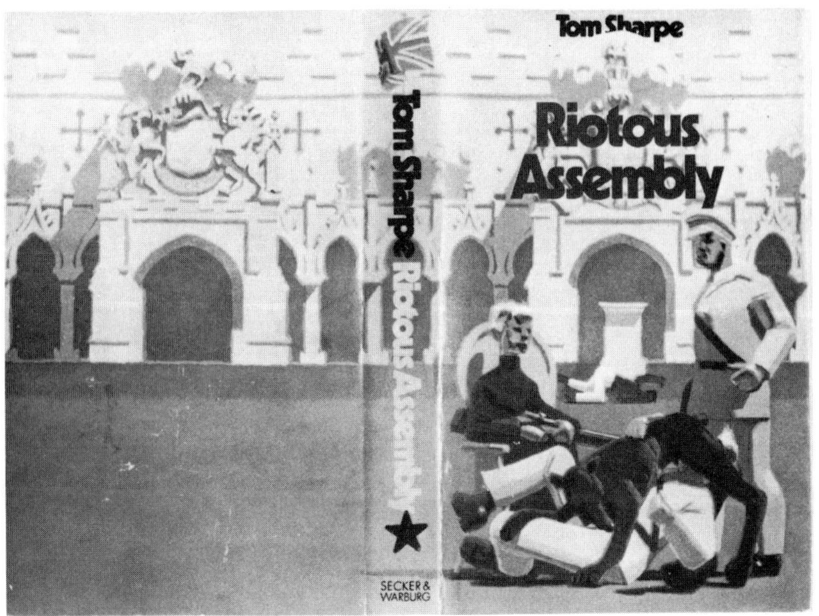

Tom Sharpe's first novel – *Riotous Assembly* (1971)

South African novelist who, in 1983, was to win the Booker Prize with *Life & Times of Michael K.* Also in 1977 appeared *The Crash of '79* by the best-selling Californian author, Paul E. Erdman.

Apart from novels, there was also Germaine Greer's *The Obstacle Race* (1979) – an account of the fortunes of women painters and their works – and the first volume of a series of essays by Hugh Trevor-Roper appeared in 1984.

After the modest success of his first novel, *Riotous Assembly* (1971), bought by Fred Warburg in 1970 after it

The first volume in the Secker & Warburg poetry series edited by Anthony Thwaite – *Cannibals and Missionaries* (1972) by John Fuller

had been submitted to Charles Latimer, then Publicity Director, Rosenthal put Tom Sharpe under a series of three-book contracts. During the life of the third of these contracts Sharpe became a substantial best-seller.

In another direction, Rosenthal was responsible for an important innovation: he engaged Anthony Thwaite as a consultant poetry editor to build a quality poetry list. Four titles appeared in 1972, including John Fuller's *Cannibals and Missionaries*.

By the time Rosenthal left the firm to take up his responsibilities at Heinemann, Secker & Warburg could no longer be described as a small, independent publishing house. Independent it certainly was, but it had become, by then, a substantial company respected for the size of its turnover as well as for the quality of the books that it brought to the public.

In 1981, Rosenthal became Chairman of William Heinemann, and moved his base of operations to Heinemann's Mayfair office. He remained Chairman of Secker & Warburg, but Peter Grose took over the day-to-day running of the firm as Publishing Director. In due course, his role at Heinemann ceased to please Rosenthal, as it took him too far from what he felt was his true function: that of a publisher. He also spent less time at the Secker offices but continued to buy books for the list – most notably Muriel St Clare Byrne's one-volume version of *The Lisle Letters* (1983) – and to preside over editorial meetings. But it was not until September 1984 that he finally resigned, and Peter Grose became Managing Director.

When Grose, a lively-minded, popular Australian, became Publishing Director in 1980, he already had a clear idea of what the firm stood for. First of all, it was international, continuing the tradition which had existed from the days of Thomas Mann, Franz Kafka, Alberto Moravia, Colette and numerous other European authors of the first rank. Secondly, it was identified with books of high quality – and with the proven ability to persuade the British public to buy them. It had a third characteristic, too, which Grose found equally sympathetic – a radical streak. It liked to stir things up, to swim against the

Muriel St Clare Byrne's abridgement of *The Lisle Letters* (1983), selected and arranged by Bridget Boland

The controversial book on the Falklands War – *The Sinking of the Belgrano* (1984) by Desmond Rice and Arthur Gavshon

current of conventional opinion. This may not have been quite as apparent as it had been during the early years of Fred Warburg's reign, but it was still there. And it was a tendency that was much to the liking of Grose who, in January 1980, came to Seckers from Curtis Brown after twelve years in the service of that eminent firm of literary agents.

Asked what might be the two events he is most proud of since he took over the direction of the business, Grose will probably say that one would be the publication of *The Sinking of the Belgrano* (1984) by Desmond Rice and

Arthur Gavshon. Rice, an executive of Shell in the Argentine, had thought of writing a novel about the Falklands War but Grose persuaded him instead to write, in collaboration with Gavshon (a former diplomatic correspondent with Associated Press), a factual book about the most dramatic incident in the war: the sinking of the Argentine cruiser *Belgrano*. *The Sinking of the Belgrano* was a good example of one kind of book which Grose, as a radical, thought Secker & Warburg should publish – the kind of book that ran counter to accepted opinion and caused a hubbub in the government. *The Sinking of the Belgrano* has so far sold 10,000 copies in hardcover alone.

Grose was even more proud to have published *The Name of the Rose* (1983) by Umberto Eco. It would be hard to describe a book less likely to be a best-seller than this one. Consider the facts: it was a first novel by an Italian Professor of Semiotics at the University of Bologna; it was set in the Middle Ages, in an abbey where mysterious goings-on had puzzled the community; it was all too obviously a learned work, the product of a mind steeped in mediaeval thought; and it had almost no women characters. 'I began writing in March of 1978,' Eco explains, 'prodded by a seminal idea. I felt like poisoning a monk.' From that germ, the story grew.

How on earth did Grose come to involve the firm in publishing such an apparently pre-destined loser? As he relates, he had sold to the Italian firm, Bompiani, the rights in a novel, *Chinese Alice* (1981), by Pat Barr, which had done well for them. Some time later, a lady telephoned him from Bompiani: 'We have published your best-seller. Why don't you publish ours?' By this time,

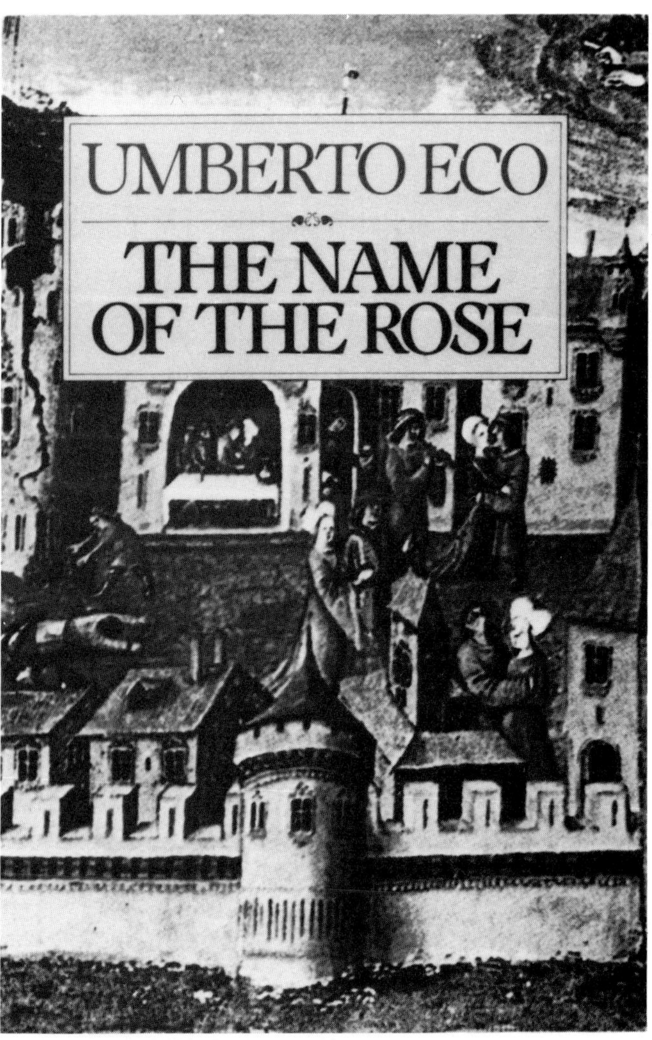

The Name of the Rose (1983) by Umberto Eco – an international bestseller

The Name of the Rose had been sold to publishers in France and Germany, but had no US or British publisher. Those who read the original were divided into the enthusiastic and the doubtful. Grose, believing the novel to be in the mainstream of Italian fiction, agreed to go ahead – he recognised the unique and extraordinary nature of the book, but had at the time no idea of its immense general appeal. When the question of sharing the heavy costs of translation with the subsequent American publisher had been settled, *The Rose* was bought for £1,000. It was an immediate success, reprinted twice before publication, and has so far sold approximately 40,000 copies in hard-cover and nearly 400,000 copies in paperback. In America it has also been a best-seller.

Anyone reading the story of Secker & Warburg will see in the publication of this remarkable novel good reason to believe that the firm is faithful to its traditions: it is international; it publishes books of high quality; it is, in the best sense of the word, unconventional.

One day in August 1985, Secker & Warburg authors received a letter which told them that the Heinemann Group, then owned by BTR after the Tillings takeover in 1983, had merged with Paul Hamlyn's Octopus Publishing Group. Paul Hamlyn was to become Chairman of the Heinemann Group, and would control the new concern. Nicolas Thompson, who had joined in March 1985 as Managing Director of the Heinemann Group, would continue as Chairman of Secker & Warburg, Peter Grose would continue as Managing Director, and John Blackwell and Gill Vale – both recruited in Fred Warburg's time – would continue as Editorial Director and Rights Director, respectively. It was the declared intention of Octopus to keep Heinemann and Secker & Warburg as autonomous publishing units. There would be no change in the publishing policy of the company.

This, then, is the latest exciting turn in a publishing story which began half a century earlier when Fredric Warburg made his bid for the moribund business of Martin Secker and thus launched Secker & Warburg on its voyage through waters that were sometimes smooth and sometimes turbulent but were always – under whatever captain – bright with the promise of adventure.

Now, having charted its course through half a century, it seems a good moment to turn the page and begin a new chapter.

A Brief Calendar of Events

1936 Fredric Warburg, formerly of George Routledge & Sons Limited, and Roger Senhouse, personal assistant to Lytton Strachey, buy the assets of Martin Secker Limited and move into Secker's offices at 5 John Street, Adelphi, London WC2. First title under the new imprint published on 4 April 1936: *Prelude to Death* by Elinor Mordaunt. Other titles include Erskine Caldwell *Tobacco Road*, Gabriel Chevallier *Clochemerle*, and Thomas Mann *Stories of Three Decades* (Mann received the Nobel Prize in 1929). Advertisement for another title, John Langdon-Davies' *Behind the Spanish Barricades*, banned by the *Observer*. Move to 22 Essex Street, Strand, London WC2, on expiry of lease.

1937 Outrage from the Left following publication of André Gide's *Back from the USSR*. Publication of Heinrich Mann *King Wren* and C. L. R. James *World Revolution, 1917–1936*.

1938 Resignation of Martin Secker to join the Richards Press. Publication of Thomas Mann *Joseph in Egypt*, George Orwell *Homage to Catalonia*, Jomo Kenyatta *Facing Mount Kenya*, Lewis Mumford *The Culture of Cities*.

1939 H. G. Wells *The Fate of Homo Sapiens*, Rayner Heppenstall *The Blaze of Noon*, V. K. Arseniev *Dersu the Trapper*, François Mauriac *Asmodée or the Intruder*.

1940 Thomas Mann *Lotte in Weimar* and *Royal Highness*, H. G. Wells *The New World Order*, *All Aboard for Ararat* and *Babes in the Darkling Wood*.

1941 William Brendon's warehouse in Plymouth bombed – 200,000 Secker & Warburg books and stock of paper destroyed. Searchlight Books series on political themes begun, edited by T. R. Fyvel and George Orwell (first title: Orwell's *The Lion and the Unicorn*). Publication of Edmund Wilson *To the Finland Station*, H. G. Wells *You Can't Be Too Careful*.

1942 Henry Miller *The Colossus of Maroussi*, Edmund Wilson *The Wound and the Bow*, H. G. Wells *The Outlook for Homo Sapiens* and *Phoenix*.

1943 Vivian Connell *The Chinese Room*, John Scott *Behind the Urals*.

1944 Essex Street offices destroyed by flying bomb, caretaker killed. Publication of Olaf Stapledon *Sirius*, Lewis Mumford *The Condition of Man*, John Prebble *Where the Sea Breaks*.

1945 Move to 7 John Street, Bloomsbury, London WC1. Publication of Franz Kafka *The Trial* (first published 1936), Thomas Mann *Joseph the Provider*, George Orwell *Animal Farm*.

1946 David Farrer joins the company from the Beaverbrook newspaper group. Sigma Books series on scientific themes (ed. Kurt Mendelssohn) begun with David S. Evans *Frontiers of Astronomy*. Publication of George Orwell *Critical Essays*, Lewis Mumford *City Development*, Gabriel Chevallier *Sainte-Colline*, Norman Douglas *South Wind* (first published 1917).

1947 André Gide receives Nobel Prize. Publication of Thomas Mann *Essays of Three Decades*, Alberto Moravia *The Fancy Dress Party*, André Gide *The Journals of André Gide* (Vol. 1), Milton Shulman *Defeat in the West*.

1948 George Orwell *Coming Up For Air* (first published 1939), André Gide *Strait is the Gate* (first published 1924) and *The Journals of André Gide* (Vol. 2), Franz Kafka *The Diaries of Franz Kafka* (Vol. 1), Lionel Trilling *The Middle of the Journey*, John Horne Burns *The Gallery*, John Prebble *Edge of Darkness*, Eric Partridge (ed.) *A Dictionary of Forces' Slang, 1939–1945*.

1949 George Orwell *Burmese Days* (first published 1935), *Nineteen Eighty-Four* and *Down and Out in Paris and London* (first published 1933), Angus Wilson *The Wrong Set*, Thomas Mann *Doctor Faustus*, Franz Kafka *The Diaries of Franz Kafka* (Vol. 2), *America* (first published 1938) and *In the Penal Settlement*, André Gide *The Journals of André Gide* (Vol. 3), Alberto Moravia *The Woman of Rome*, Oliver Lawson Dick (ed.) *Aubrey's Brief Lives*, Eric Partridge *Name Into Word*.

1950 Angus Wilson *Such Darling Dodos*, André Gide *If It Die*, George Orwell *Shooting an Elephant*, Hervé Bazin *Grasping the Viper*.

1951 Secker & Warburg join the Heinemann Group (finalised 1952). Publication of André Gide *The Journals of André Gide* (Vol. 4), Colette *Chéri*, James A. Michener *Return to Paradise*, Lionel Trilling *The Liberal Imagination*.

1952 Angus Wilson *Hemlock and After*, Dino Buzzati *The Tartar Steppe*, Alberto Moravia *The Conformist*, J. L. Talmon *The Origins of Totalitarian Democracy*.

1953 First issue of *Encounter* literary magazine distributed from Secker & Warburg offices, edited by Stephen Spender. Publication of Robert Musil *The Man Without Qualities* (Vol. 1), Alberto Moravia *The Time of Indifference*, Colette *Gigi and the Cat*, John Wain *Hurry on Down*, James A. Michener *The Bridges at Toko-Ri*, Czeslaw Milosz *The Captive Mind*, Stanley Kauffman *The Philanderer*.

1954 Stanley Kauffman's *The Philanderer* prosecuted for obscene libel (acquitted). Publication of George Orwell *Keep the Aspidistra Flying* (first published 1936), Pierre Boulle *The Bridge on the River Kwai*, Christy Brown *My Left Foot*, Robert Musil *The Man Without Qualities* (Vol. 2), André Malraux *The Voices of Silence*, Michael St John Packe *The Life of John Stuart Mill*, Richard Bissell *A Gross of Pyjamas* (basis of 'The Pajama Game'), Roald Dahl *Someone Like You*.

1955 First Japanese novel published by Secker & Warburg: Jiro Osaragi *Homecoming*. Publication of Marguerite Yourcenar *Memoirs of Hadrian*, Robert Musil *Young Törless*, Thomas Mann *The Confessions of Felix Krull*, Norman Douglas *Old Calabria* (first published 1915).

1956 Publication and subsequent controversy regarding authenticity of hoax autobiography *The Third Eye* by 'T. Lobsang Rampa'. Publication of Tennessee Williams *Cat on a Hot Tin Roof*, Roger Fenton *L. J. M. Daguerre*, Thomas Mann *Joseph and his Brothers*, Angus Wilson *Anglo-Saxon Attitudes*, Alberto Moravia *Roman Tales*, Junichiro Tanizaki *Some Prefer Nettles*, Norman St John Stevas *Obscenity and the Law*, Eric Newby *The Last Grain Race*, Natalia Ginzburg *Dead Yesterdays*, David Beaty *The Proving Flight*, Colette *Claudine at School*, J. R. Ackerley *My Dog Tulip*, Angus Heriot *The Castrati in Opera*, D. J. Enright *Bread Rather than Blossoms*.

1957 Angus Wilson *A Bit off the Map*, Marguerite Yourcenar *Coup de Grâce*, Roger Peyrefitte *The Keys of St Peter*, Nathanael West *The Complete Works of Nathanael West*, Yukio Mishima *The Sound of Waves* and *Five Modern Nō Plays*, Yasunari Kawabata *Snow Country*, Norman Cohn *The Pursuit of the Millenium*, Shohei Ooka *Fires on the Plain*, Raymond Aron *The Opium of the Intellectuals*.

1958 Writers at Work series, collections of interviews with writers from the *Paris Review*, begun (first series edited by

Malcolm Cowley). Knockout Thrillers series begun with Evelyn Piper's *Bunny Lake is Missing*. Publication of Junichiro Tanizaki *The Makioka Sisters*, Alberto Moravia *Two Women*, Eric Newby *A Short Walk in the Hindu Kush*, Angus Wilson *The Middle Age of Mrs Eliot*, Colette *Stories of Colette*, Sylvia Ashton-Warner *Spinster*, Edgar Mittelholzer *Kaywana Blood*, Jan Carew *Black Midas*, Christopher Hill *Puritanism and Revolution*, Christine Brooke-Rose *A Grammar of Metaphor*, John Prebble *My Great-Aunt Appearing Day*, Frank Norman *Bang to Rights*.

1959 Malcolm Bradbury *Eating People is Wrong*, Federico García Lorca *Tragedies*, George Orwell *The Road to Wigan Pier* (first published 1937), David Beaty *Cone of Silence*, Yasunari Kawabata *Thousand Cranes*, Nikos Kazantzakis *The Odyssey*, John Knowles *A Separate Peace*.

1960 Thomas Tilling Group take over Heinemann Group including Secker & Warburg. Publication of James A. Michener *Hawaii*, David Daiches *A Critical History of English Literature*, William L. Shirer *The Rise and Fall of the Third Reich*, Robert Musil *The Man Without Qualities* (Vol. 3), Malcolm Cowley (ed.) *Walt Whitman's Leaves of Grass*, Clancy Sigal *Weekend in Dinlock*.

1961 Move to 14 Carlisle Street, Soho, London W1. Mercury Books paperback imprint begun in association with William Heinemann and Hart-Davis – first title Fred Hoyle's *Frontiers of Astronomy*. Albatross Guides, a series of travel guides (ed. Herbert Spencer), begun with *Crete* by John Bowman. Reporter series (later renamed History in the Making) – eye-witness accounts of great events in history – begun under editorship of Georges Pernoud with *The French Revolution* by Georges Pernoud and Sabine Flaissier. Britain Alive series (eds Clancy Sigal and Mervyn Jones) on aspects of life in contemporary Britain begun with Mervyn Jones' *Potbank*. Publication of George Orwell *Collected Essays*,

Junichiro Tanizaki *The Key*, Angus Wilson *The Old Men at the Zoo*, John Barth *The Sot-Weed Factor*, Alberto Moravia *The Empty Canvas*, Sefton Delmer *Trail Sinister*, Isaac Bashevis Singer *The Magician of Lublin*, Lewis Mumford *The City in History*, John Prebble *Culloden*, André Schwarz-Bart *The Last of the Just*.

1962 Roger Senhouse resigns. Publication of Italo Svevo *Confessions of Zeno* (first published 1930), Günter Grass *The Tin Drum*, Tennessee Williams *Five Plays*, Oscar Lewis *The Children of Sánchez*.

1963 Günter Grass *Cat and Mouse*, Alberto Moravia *More Roman Tales*, Julian Gloag *Our Mother's House*, Dennis Gabor *Inventing the Future*, John Prebble *The Highland Clearances*.

1964 August Strindberg *The Plays* (Vol. 1), Pierre Boulle *Monkey Planet*, Angus Wilson *Late Call*, Paul Scott *The Corrida at San Felíu*, Brigid Brophy *Hackenfeller's Ape* (first published 1953).

1965 Margaret Forster *Georgy Girl*, Malcolm Bradbury *Stepping Westward*, Kobo Abé *The Woman in the Dunes*, August Strindberg *From an Occult Diary*, James A. Michener *The Source*, Günter Grass *Dog Years*, Melvyn Bragg *For Want of a Nail*, Federico García Lorca *Five Plays*, G. A. Williamson (ed.) *Foxe's Book of Martyrs*.

1966 Alan Ross/London Magazine Editions titles distributed by Secker & Warburg. Publication of Yukio Mishima *The Sailor Who Fell From Grace with the Sea*, Christina Stead *The Man Who Loved Children*, Arthur Miller *The Crucible* (first published 1956) and *Incident at Vichy*, Ilsa Barea *Vienna: Legend and Reality*, B. S. Johnson *Trawl*, Erich Heller *The Artist's Journey into the Interior*, Colette *Earthly Paradise*, Adam B. Ulam *Lenin and the Bolsheviks*.

1967 Barley Alison joins the company from Weidenfeld &

Nicolson to form The Alison Press. Cinema One series begun in association with the British Film Institute – trade paperbacks on films and film-makers edited by Penelope Houston, Tom Milne and Peter Wollen (first title *Jean-Luc Godard* by Richard Roud). Publication of John Barth *Giles Goat-Boy*, Arthur Miller *Collected Plays*, Christina Stead *Cotters' England*, Angus Wilson *No Laughing Matter*, Dennis Bloodworth *Chinese Looking Glass*, Italo Svevo *Short Sentimental Journey*, Jim Philip, John Simpson and Nicholas Snowman (eds) *The Best of Granta, 1889–1966*, Roger Peyrefitte *The Jews*, Kitty Muggeridge and Ruth Adam *Beatrice Webb*.

1968 Maurice Temple Smith resigns as Managing Director. Yasunari Kawabata awarded Nobel Prize. Publication of Yukio Mishima *Forbidden Colours*, James A. Michener *Iberia*, Piers Paul Read *The Junkers*, Boris Pasternak *Letters to Georgian Friends*, George Orwell *Collected Essays, Journalism and Letters*, J. L. Carr *A Season in Sinji*, John Ardagh *The New French Revolution*.

1969 World Realities series, edited by Brian Crozier, begun with Max Beloff's *The Future of British Foreign Policy*. Publication of August Strindberg *The Cloister*, James A. Michener *Sayonara*.

1970 Angus Wilson *The World of Charles Dickens*, Thomas Mann *Letters of Thomas Mann*, Christy Brown *Down All the Days*, Günter Grass *Local Anaesthetic*.

1971 Fredric Warburg retires, Tom Rosenthal joins from Thames & Hudson as Managing Director. Dennis Gabor receives Nobel Prize for Physics. History of London series begun with George Rudé's *Hanoverian London*. Cinema Two series on historical and critical writing on the cinema begun with Alistair Cooke (ed.) *Garbo and the Night Watchmen* (first published 1937). Publication of Tom Sharpe *Riotous Assembly*, Yukio Mishima *Sun & Steel*, James A.

Michener *The Drifters*, Masuji Ibuse *Black Rain*, Bryan Magee *Modern British Philosophy*.

1972 Heinrich Böll awarded Nobel Prize. Secker & Warburg Poets series, edited by Anthony Thwaite, begun with John Fuller *Cannibals and Missionaries.* Leo Baeck Institute proceedings published for first time under Secker & Warburg imprint. Publication of Graham Greene *The Pleasure-Dome*, George V. Higgins *The Friends of Eddie Coyle*, Michael Ayrton *Fabrications*, David Cook *Albert's Memorial*.

1973 Charles Pick becomes Chairman of Secker & Warburg. Publication of Yasunari Kawabata *The Master of Go*, Heinrich Böll *Group Portrait With Lady*, *And Where Were You, Adam?*, *Children Are Civilians Too* and *The Train Was On Time*, August Strindberg *A Dream Play*, Dudley Pope *Governor Ramage RN*, Wyndham Lewis *The Roaring Queen*, Yukio Mishima *Runaway Horses*, John Rewald *The History of Impressionism*.

1974 Robert Penn Warren *All the King's Men* (first published 1948), James A. Michener *Centennial*, Arthur Miller *Focus*, Erica Jong *Fear of Flying*, Tom Sharpe *Porterhouse Blue*, Günter Grass *From the Diary of a Snail*, Piers Paul Read *Alive*, Carl Bernstein and Bob Woodward *All the President's Men*, Alfred Döblin *Alexanderplatz* (first published 1931), Italo Calvino *Invisible Cities*, Malcolm Easton and Michael Holroyd *The Art of Augustus John*.

1975 David Lodge *Changing Places*, Tom Sharpe *Blott on the Landscape*, Saul Bellow *Humboldt's Gift*, Heinrich Böll *The Lost Honour of Katharina Blum*, Malcolm Bradbury *The History Man*, Stanislaw Lem *The Cyberiad*, Maurice Leitch *Stamping Ground*, David Thomson *A Biographical Dictionary of the Cinema*, August Strindberg *The Plays* (Vol. 2).

1976 Saul Bellow awarded Nobel Prize. Publication of Tom Sharpe *Wilt*, Malcolm Bradbury *Who Do You Think You Are?*, Murasaki Shikibu *The Tale of Genji*, John Banville

Doctor Copernicus, Mark Holloway *Norman Douglas*, Federico García Lorca *Collected Plays*, Heinrich Böll *The Bread of Those Early Years*, Melvyn Bragg *Speak for England*.

1977 Guy Bellamy *The Secret Lemonade Drinker*, Paul E. Erdman *The Crash of '79*, Heinrich Böll *Missing Persons*, Tom Sharpe *The Great Pursuit*, Italo Calvino *The Castle of Crossed Destinies*, Erica Jong *How to Save Your Own Life*, J. M. Coetzee *In the Heart of the Country*, Carlos Fuentes *Terra Nostra* and *The Death of Artemio Cruz* (first published 1964), P. N. Furbank *E. M. Forster* (Vol. 1), A. N. Wilson *The Sweets of Pimlico*, Arthur Drexler (ed.) *The Architecture of the Ecole Des Beaux-Arts*.

1978 Move to 54 Poland Street, Soho, London W1. Publication of David Cook *Walter*, Tom Sharpe *The Throwback*, P. N. Furbank *E. M. Forster* (Vol. 2), Hugh Trevor-Roper (ed.) *The Goebbels Diaries*, Barrie Penrose and Roger Courtiour *The Pencourt File*, Heinrich Böll *And Never Said A Word* (first published 1955), James A. Michener *Chesapeake*, Günter Grass *The Flounder* and *In the Egg*.

1979 Tom Sharpe *The Wilt Alternative*, Gordon Rattray Taylor *The Natural History of the Mind*, Germaine Greer *The Obstacle Race*, Piers Brendon *Eminent Edwardians*, James Melville *The Wages of Zen*, Nicholas Mosley *Catastrophe Practice*.

1980 Peter Grose joins Secker & Warburg from Curtis Brown as Publishing Director. Czeslaw Milosz awarded Nobel Prize. Publication of Bernard Crick *George Orwell: A Life*, Angus Wilson *Setting the World on Fire*, John Barth *Letters*, J. M. Coetzee *Waiting for the Barbarians*, Tom Sharpe *Ancestral Vices*, George Malcolm Thomson *The Prime Ministers*, Ronald Haver *David O. Selznick's Hollywood*, James A. Michener *The Covenant*, David Lodge *How Far Can You Go?*

1981 Tom Rosenthal becomes Chairman of William Heinemann and of Secker & Warburg. Publication of John Banville *Kepler*, Pat Barr *Chinese Alice*, Günter Grass *The Meeting at Telgte*, Michael Moorcock *Byzantium Endures*, Italo Calvino *If On A Winter's Night A Traveller*, Yevgeny Yevtushenko *Invisible Threads*, A. Conan Doyle *The Complete Sherlock Holmes*, Raleigh Trevelyan *Rome '44*, Maurice Leitch *Silver's City*.

1982 Leo Cooper military books first published under Secker & Warburg imprint. History of Parliament series begun in association with the History of Parliament Trust (general editor P. W. Hasler). Publication of Heinrich Böll *The Safety Net*, Saul Bellow *The Dean's December*, Günter Grass *Headbirths*, A. N. Wilson *Wise Virgin*, James A. Michener *Space*, Tom Sharpe *Vintage Stuff*, Nicholas Mosley *Rules of the Game*, Kitagawa Utamaro *A Chorus of Birds*, J. M. Coetzee *Dusklands*, Ursula Bentley *The Natural Order*.

1983 J. M. Coetzee *Life & Times of Michael K*, Malcolm Bradbury *Rates of Exchange*, Heinrich Böll *Irish Journal*, William Least Heat Moon *Blue Highways*, Italo Calvino *Marcovaldo* and *Difficult Loves*, Umberto Eco *The Name of the Rose*, Muriel St Clare Byrne (ed.) *The Lisle Letters*, Alberto Moravia *1934*, James A. Michener *Poland*, A. F. N. Clarke *Contact*, Melvyn Bragg *Land of the Lakes*, Pat Barr *Uncut Jade*, Günter Grass *Drawings and Words 1954–1977*, Alan Brownjohn *Collected Poems 1952–83*, Yousuf Karsh *Karsh*.

1984 Tom Rosenthal resigns from Heinemann Group and Secker & Warburg, Peter Grose becomes Managing Director of Secker & Warburg. Publication of Cynthia Ozick *The Cannibal Galaxy*, Desmond Rice and Arthur Gavshon *The Sinking of the Belgrano*, Germaine Greer *Sex and Destiny*, David Lodge *Small World*, Ann Thwaite *Edmund Gosse*, Saul Bellow *Him With His Foot In His Mouth*, George Orwell *Nineteen Eighty-Four: The Facsimile of the Extant Manuscript*, Robert Phelps (ed.) *The Collected Stories of Colette*, Michael

Moorcock *The Laughter of Carthage*, August Strindberg *By the Open Sea*, Kitagawa Utamaro *Songs of the Garden*, John Prebble *John Prebble's Scotland*, Anthony Thwaite *Poems 1953–1983*, David Hooper *Public Scandal, Odium and Contempt*, Tom Sharpe *Wilt on High*, John Strawson *A History of the SAS Regiment*, Hugh Trevor-Roper *Religion, the Reformation and Social Change* (first published 1967).

1985 Octopus Group take over Heinemann Group including Secker & Warburg. Charles Pick retires. Nicolas Thompson joins from Pitman as Managing Director of the Heinemann Group and Chairman of Secker & Warburg. Publication of James A. Michener *Texas*, David Thomson *Suspects*, Robert Walshe *Wales' Work*, Yukio Mishima *The Sea of Fertility*, Hugh Trevor-Roper *Renaissance Essays*, Heinrich Böll *What's to Become of the Boy?* and *A Soldier's Legacy*, Jacob Burckhardt *Architecture of the Italian Renaissance*, Italo Calvino *Mr Palomar*, Alberto Moravia *Erotic Tales*, Pat Barr *Kenjiro*, Flora Fraser (ed.) *Maud: The Diaries of Maud Berkeley*, Roy Fuller *New and Collected Poems 1934–84*, Michael Meyer *Strindberg*, Günter Grass *On Writing and Politics, 1967–1983*, Colin Seymour-Ure and Jim Schoff *David Low*, John Fuller *Selected Poems 1954–82*, Julian Thompson *No Picnic*, Roy McMullen *Degas*.